Family Values Series

Responsibilities

of

Fathers

TORKOM
SARAYDARIAN

**T.S.G. Publishing
Foundation, Inc.**

Responsibilities of Fathers
Excerpted from *Sex, Family, and the Woman in Society,* (Ch. 35.)

Copyright 1999, The Creative Trust

ISBN: 0-929874-71-4
LOC# *Sex, Family and the Woman in Society* 86-71759
Printed in the United States of America

Published by:

    T.S.G. Publishing Foundation, Inc.
    PO Box 7068
    Cave Creek, AZ 85327-7068
    USA

Note: Spiritual information contained herein is given as a guideline. They should be used with descretion and after recieving professional advice.

Published by the generous donations to the
Torkom Saraydarian Book Publishing Fund

Responsibilities of Fathers

The father is very important in the life of his child. It is the presence of the father that builds the mental body of his child. Many children do not have fathers, and many children have fathers but do not live with them. Many children have fathers who are not interested in them. Thus there is a great vacuum in the souls of these children.

Naturally, children try to substitute their nonexistent, absent, or indifferent fathers with another father figure, such as an uncle, brother, teacher, or priest. But in their souls, the children crave their fathers. Once a seven-year-old boy told me he missed his father who had divorced his mother and was living in another state. "What do you really miss?" I asked.

"I miss his hand holding my hand in hiking." And tears came from his eyes.

"Well," I said, trying to comfort him, "your new father likes you and gives you whatever you wish to have."

"But I miss my real father and his hand."

There was a deep wound in his heart, and wiping his eyes with his little hands he whispered to me, "But don't say anything to Mommy.

Years passed. He was a lonely boy. One day, when he was eighteen, we met at a party. "You look great," I said, hugging him.

"You know," he said, "I am living with my father now. He taught me to stand on my own feet. Something is complete in me. I don't know what it is, but I feel complete."

What are the responsibilities of a Father?

1. **Building his children's mental bodies is a father's first responsibility.** A father has a great responsibility to make his children feel complete. This feeling of completeness is the building of the mental body.

A mother does not build her children's mental bodies. She builds their emotional and intuitional bodies. That is why the presence of both the father and mother in a loving relationship with each other is essential to the psychological construction of the child.

One of the reasons there is so much teenage crime and suicide is the absence of the father, or the absence of his wisdom, caring, and noble presence. Another reason for teenage crime and suicide is that the child becomes disoriented when his father is substituted by other men. When a child's mother changes husbands or boyfriends, it confuses the child, leaving a bad scar in his mental body.

Each child needs a masculine presence in order to build himself. Preferably, it should be a presence that is related to his blood and bones. If this is not possible, the role of the masculine presence can be filled by a close teacher, priest, or doctor. A boy needs his own masculinity to be affirmed and noticed by his father. A girl needs to develop the masculine side of her nature in order to balance her life. Both boys and girls look to their father in the process of building their minds and personalities.

For a boy, his father is the present. For a girl, her father is the future. The image of her father will play a great role in a girl intelligently choosing her boyfriends and her future partner.

An absent father for a girl will be an absent man, even though she marries a fine husband. To her, the man in her husband will be absent and she will always continue to look, openly or secretly, for the man or father that she did not have. This is a cause of many problems that women who were raised without their fathers have.

A father always builds the masculine standard in the child. If this standard is not built during childhood, it will be extremely difficult to build a standard later by artificial means of education.

What a father essentially is, is his beingness. The father's beingness is more than just what he says and does. That beingness is what is taken by the child as his standard. The process of a child absorbing the father's beingness to build his standards is very subtle. The father's conversations, thoughts, and acts all evoke the construction of the child's mental body. The father's example of striving, courage, daring, patience, diplomacy, and the way he handles problems, inspires his child to build his mental body according to that example.

3

A wise father not only builds a high standard but also makes that standard flexible and ready to grow and expand by the efforts the child makes in the future.

Many years later, when you examine the basic character of children built under varied influences, you will always find at the foundation the standards built by their fathers. If the mental body of the child is not built, he turns into a problem. He cannot decide for himself, he cannot plan, and he has no firm goals. He becomes like a butterfly flitting from one flower to another. He cannot solve problems. He turns into an effect rather than a cause, and he lets people use or exploit him in various ways.

The condition of the child worsens if he is talented. He wastes his talents and uses them for his lower pleasures or the pleasures of others. Such children can be called "mental abortions," because they have had the construction of their mental bodies thwarted.

Many children are born with talent, with many great tendencies for art, for politics, for science. But if the father is absent, or if the substitute father is not totally accepted by the child, the child's mental body will be weak. Every time a responsibility is given to such a child, he will escape it because he does not have a responsible example impressed in his mind.

A father's example turns into a hidden, dynamic force that controls the decisions of the child according to the degree and depth of the impression.

If a child lives only with his mother, his emotional and intuitional bodies will be built, but not his mental body. If the mental body is not built in a young person who is intuitive, he will become non-realistic, dreamy, too abstract and impractical, without common sense or the ability to translate emotions and intuitive impressions into workable patterns. Such a person cannot fit himself to society and the environment, or he eventually becomes the tool of those who know how to manipulate others.

If a man did not have a real father when he was growing up, or if he had a substitute father who was not real for him, when he marries he psychologically becomes the child of his wife, rather than her husband. If a woman did not have a real father when she was growing up, when she marries she becomes the child of her husband in her psychology. Such relationships do not last long or may end with tragedy.

On the other hand, if a child is raised only by his father, his mind will be developed, but not his emotions or intuition. Without developed heart qualities, the mind is a danger for him and for society.

The mind is meant to actualize inspirations, visions, and feelings coming from the intuitional and emotional bodies and to turn them into concrete forms to be used for the betterment of human living.

At the present time, many women are assuming the role of both father and mother. This is sometimes presented as the liberation of women. Many women already are more masculine than feminine, and they reject men who do not support their masculine lifestyle.

A child raised by such a masculine mother is either confused or accepts his mother as his masculine role model and copies her as he tries to develop his incomplete mental nature even if his father lives with him.

Many fathers also now try to be mother and father, and this disturbs the deep-seated instincts of the child, causing negative physical and psychological effects.

A child must know that he has a father and a mother, that they are different from each other and have different responsibilities toward him. In certain things the child must relate with his father; in other things he must relate with his mother. Both mother and father must contribute in their own unique ways to the construction of the child's complete nature.

There is deep confusion in the hearts of our children. Most of them do not have a decent family life. Their father is not there. Another man is there. Two months later, another man is there, then another man, and then another. The children cannot figure out what to do. Many men are impressed into their half-built mental equipment, each with different characteristics. They do not know what the standard is.

On the other hand, daddy is running after another woman. Every month or year he has another woman living with him. The child cannot build his heart, his emotions or his intuitional body in such confusion. It seems to him that daddy and mommy are out of their minds and not in their hearts. Instability builds its nest in the child's character.

Many men and women in high positions in society act like children or teenagers because of the standards they copied from their parents. Sometimes the destiny of large numbers of people are in the hands of such immature, confused people. You read about a judge running away with a teenage girl, or a politician using in his international relations the same games he used to play with his friends. You read about a wealthy woman stealing the diamond of another woman.

When people grow in body and rise in position without being psychologically mature, the result will be increasing crime and unhappiness in their families and in society as a whole, with long-range consequences.

A teenage girl with tears in her eyes once told me, "I love my father, but every time I get the courage to talk to him and hug him, he takes fifty dollars out of his wallet and gives it to me. I go away with a deep vacuum in my heart. I need his hugs, his presence, his respect; they make me feel more solid, more together. I don't need his money, but that's all he gives me." This girl will search for a father in another man to give her the solidity she needs.

The father image in the psychology of a child is stability, solidity, leadership, daring, courage, firmness, making visions practical, sacrificing for achievements, being a refuge and protection, understanding the problems of life, and giving direction.

A child feels that he owns his father, and if he sees any kind of faltering or nonsense in his father, the development of his mental body is impaired.

A child must not think, "Who is my father? Who is my mother? Why are they not together?" Such thoughts have a very frustrating influence in his mind.

Lucky are those children who early in life discover the instability of their homes and search for a stable relationship in which to build their psychological foundations. If they find someone to give them the example and essence they need to complete their mental bodies or emotional and intuitional bodies, they will have a future.

The foundation on which a family must be built to create psychologically-together children is self-sacrifice. If the mother and father do not stand on this foundation, failures in life are perpetuated.

2. **The second responsibility of a father is to evoke willpower in his children.** Many children are just like jellyfish, without backbones and swayed by every current. They lack willpower and the urge and drive to reach heights of achievement. They wait for people to tell them what to do and how to do it. Willpower is an inner direction that makes a person initiate action and overcome obstacles in the process of the action.

Fathers who are manly, masculine, and full of striving and courage produce children who go far in their evolution and fields of achievement. To be a father, one needs to have had a real father himself. If the chain of real fatherhood is broken, you will have broken links and half-fathers.

My Father used to say that if a father is not a real father, the children's clay remains loose and does not take shape or retain any "solid" form.

The father's willpower is not a force that he imposes on his children, nor is it the imposition of his own likes and dislikes. Real willpower never imposes itself but evokes the willpower in others to bloom the way they want to bloom. Such willpower makes children dare to become courageous and decisive, to climb toward greater achievements.

3. **The third fundamental responsibility of a father is to provide financial support to his children** — to let them eat well, dress well, have a good home, go to good schools and colleges, and enjoy the beauties of Nature in various ways. Those fathers who want to have children without providing for their basic needs are committing a great mistake because they will be the ones who will pay the karma of their children.

Willpower and the mental body can be developed in children if the father gives time for it, using the following simple methods:

a. *The father takes his children hiking in the mountains.* He then is an example of many qualities, such as courage, carefulness, creative movements, caution, endurance, joyfulness, and the ability to solve problems.

While hiking and climbing in the mountains he must not show off but be with them to watch their steps and show by example how to surpass difficulties and unexpected hindrances. Children who climb mountains in such a way learn how to climb to spiritual, social, and moral heights.

I have watched many children climb with teachers, friends, uncles, and brothers. They enjoy it, but it is a totally different experience when they climb with their fathers. The experience is more fiery, more real, more emotional, more heartfelt, more enthusiastic. No one can replace a father for a child.

b. *The father climbs trees, showing his children how to do the seemingly "impossible."* The purpose is to give them an example of making "impossible" things possible, showing how the difficult is conquerable. "If Daddy can climb, so can I," the child will say.

The failure of fathers to do seemingly difficult things is a psychological failure for the child. For a child, climbing mountains or trees is not exactly climbing mountains and trees. They are psychological events in his soul, symbols in his mind that can be activated at any moment in his later life when he needs inspiration, help, or a solution to a problem.

For example, Daddy crossed the river and stood on the other bank with a smile of victory. Such a picture in a child's mind will be a source of inspiration in the future during difficult hours when he is faced with "rough currents" of problems and crises. In his mind, the child will see his father's image suggesting victory. It will tell him to be courageous and daring, that the other shore can be conquered and problems can be solved.

c. *A father must take his children for walks in the nighttime, when it is really dark.* He can take them to the deserts, mountains, or ocean shores, or to small villages where there are no electric lights, and show them stars, constellations, the silhouettes of mountains and trees, or the shining waves in the ocean or river. He must show how he is not afraid in darkness, and how he dressed properly and prepared for any surprise event or danger. He must teach them to be careful and cautious, but fearless. The father must not say, "Do not be afraid; there is nothing in darkness," because there are many dangers in darkness. Instead, he must teach his children how to confront dangers and surprises.

Experiences in the darkness will remain in the hearts of his children, and in future years walking in darkness will be a symbol of overcoming fears, ignorance, anxieties, worries, and confusion. The children will be able to handle the darkness of life because they already did with Daddy.

d. *The father must do work with his children,* such as gardening, planting trees, building, repairing, and fixing plumbing so that in the future the children can do these things. Such labor develops the children's mental bodies. The mental body is developed when one confronts a problem and tries to solve it in the best way possible.

The child must be involved with his father in all construction activities. A child looks to his father as his future. The future must be kept beneficial and noble in the child's eyes so that the child does not lose his hope and his urge to reach out. If the father cannot repair a window, change a washer in the faucet, build a doghouse, or pour a little cement, his child does not lose faith in his father, but he loses faith in his own future.

A friend of mine studied car repair for two years in classes, and you should see the joy his children have when he repairs broken cars, making them run like new. One day I asked him, "'Why don't you take your cars to the garage for repairs? You have enough money."

He responded, "I repair cars only to involve my children and to teach them how they can do things themselves instead of waiting for others to do things for them."

The experiences of building, constructing, and repairing things are transformed in children's psyches. In the future, they can use such experiences to "build," to "repair" constructive activities, to write books, and to compose music.

One of my musical compositions reflects an experience I had as a youth. I worked six months as an iron smith, beating red-hot iron on the anvil with heavy hammers alongside four other workers. The rhythm of hammering penetrated into my soul, and years later became the rhythm of a piece of music.

Everything is a symbol for a child. When a child's father and mother are fighting, for him the planets and stars in the Universe are fighting. A child's soul is multidimensional, and each experience is a symbol easily translated in many ways and kept in the secret chamber of his heart to be used in determining how he will act in the future. For example, when in the future he sees a man and woman employee fighting in his office, he feels the same anxiety as when his mother and father were fighting.

Adults in general are not multidimensional because they are firmly locked in their brain consciousness. But a child is still in his emotional and mental spheres.

e. *A child must see his father as a hero, doing heroic deeds.* A father shows his child that he is a hero through his right actions, his emotional confidence, his mental decisions, and his noble relationships with others. One heroic action by the father reechoes in the life of his child until the end of his life. The child believes that because his father can do such great things, he can also. But the child must be taught the needed preparations and the needed knowledge to do such actions. This stimulates his mind to learn and grow.

When a child looks to his father as his hero and the father does cowardly or sneaky things, he hurts the child, paralyzing his striving.

In one of the schools where I studied as a youth, we had a guard who once left the gate open and a horse ran away. The Teacher called the guard to the office. He came with his eight-year old son. Seeing the child, the Teacher changed his expression. He smiled and hugged the man and son. "My boy," he said to the child, "if you go and count how many goats we have, I will be grateful to you." When the boy left, the Teacher turned to the guard and, giving him a stern look, said, "I thought I could trust you. You will not return to the school until you bring back the horse, and after that I know what to do with you."

The guard said, "Yes, I was not doing my task." And he went out to search for the horse.

When he left, I asked the Teacher, "Why did you send the boy to count goats that do not exist? We do not have any goats here now. They are out with the shepherd."

"Well," he said, "children must not know about the failures of their fathers. It wounds them, and sometimes to heal such a wound is not easy."

You can read on the front pages of daily newspapers what horrible things fathers and mothers do. The respect of children toward such parents evaporates. Even if children know about the failure of their father, they do not want others to know about it because their father is their pride. Also, a child interprets the failure of any father as the failure of his own father. If you kill such pride in a child, you kill the foundation of the child. That is why it is very harmful and even criminal to humiliate a father or a mother in the presence of their child.

After divorce certain women talk very badly about their husbands to justify themselves to their children. But with all his failures, his children still love him as their father. He is their hero, even if he is a bum. Similarly, when husbands humiliate the image of their wives in front of the children, they destroy the foundation of the children, causing them eventually to become problems for society.

It is possible that the father and mother are rotten, but there are many other ways to explain a divorce to the children or to handle disagreements without destroying the foundation of the children.

I had a grandmother who was the mediator of many relatives and generations in our family. When no one else could settle disputes or angry relationships, she would speak to the people involved. One of her techniques was to build up the image of the husband and wife in each other's minds and create respect and trust between them. She saved many marriages and the children of those marriages.

A father is the hero of his child. That image must be kept alive in the child if he is to grow psychologically healthy. A father's heroic deeds are a constant source of joy and pure pride for his child, and they impress him to do greater things than his father. A father's heroic deeds build in his child the foundation of self-respect. Self-respect is the substance that builds identity and the mental body. A problem child is one who has no self-respect. If a child loses self-respect or respect for his father, the downfall of that child begins.

The psyche of the father lives in the child. A child's experiences with his father deeply influence his soul.

f. *A father must involve his children in discovering solutions to problems,* such as, what should be done when the dog is sick, when the trees in the yard are dying, when the roof is leaking, when the electricity has short-circuited, or when the computer is not working. With efforts to find solutions to such problems, the mental body of the child grows. Also, his willpower increases when he works with his father to solve problems. Some-times children come up with amazing solutions, and this gives them great joy.

Often a father should let his child try to solve problems by himself, in his presence, or with some advice if necessary. As the child's confidence increases in solving problems, his mental body develops and searches for new problems to solve.

Many high school and college youths are lost in the problems of life. Their fathers need to discuss problems with them and help them find possible solutions, so they will not turn to the "solutions" of alcohol, drugs, or destructive music.

g. *A father should teach his children self-sufficiency.* He can encourage them to do things by themselves and to learn to depend on themselves. Self-sufficiency can be taught easily by taking the child to the wilderness with little or no supplies. There the father can demonstrate what to do in case of various dangers such as snakebites, scorpions, bears, lack of pure water, getting lost, blizzards, and so on. He can demonstrate what to do to find and prepare food, how to make a shelter, how to tell directions, how to find water, and so on.

Nowadays, when a family goes to the mountains or camping, they take a van loaded with every kind of food and drink. The mother works from morning to night feeding and cleaning up, and the family spends all their time eating and drinking.

A child needs to experience a feeling of being "left alone," with the love and confidence of his parents. Such an experience will help him not to depend on others and not to be a burden or a load on the shoulders of others.

When we create too much comfort and luxury for children, we prevent their minds from growing.

   h. *A father must show his children how to serve others without expectations.* A friend of mine who had two sons used to mow the lawns of old people in the neighborhood and have his sons help. Those boys used to feel such joy when the old ladies would hug them and thank them for their service. What a blessing that father was to his sons.

   Another friend of mine used to stop and help motorists who were stranded with flat tires. One day his young daughter was with him when he stopped to help a young woman. His daughter helped change the tire, and the woman said, "My goodness, if your twelve-year-old daughter can change a tire, why can't I?" (Evidently her father had never taught her.) When a child learns to serve others in small things, he will serve greater national and international needs in the future without seeking his own self-interest. Service to others without expectation cultivates and develops the mind in the right direction.

   i. *A father can take his children horseback-riding.* Children learn much in the process of riding horses. Those people who know how to ride horses have developed a conquering spirit and a well-balanced, stable mind. The horse does not remain as a horse in the mind of the child, but it becomes his own body or a class or an army, which he can control, direct, and lead.

In learning how to control a horse, a child learns how to control his own body, emotions, and mind. There are many simple events or situations in which a child often loses control. But if he learns how to control a horse, he can control the events or situations.

One day a neighbor boy asked his father to take him horseback-riding. "Horseback-riding!" exclaimed his father. "Why horseback-riding? I will take you to dinner and you can eat whatever you want. Or I will take you to the circus to see the clowns." The boy was disappointed and sat in the garage the rest of the day.

Actually, it was not the horseback-riding that the boy wanted. It was much deeper than that. The boy wanted to prove to himself that he could handle something bigger than himself. A horse is not a horse for a child. A horse is a challenge. If he can ride a horse, he can also handle any big problem with ease. The experience of horseback-riding in the life of a child is translated in many ways, and in each translation the child is challenged for victory.

j. *A father must teach his children to be able to face the negative conditions of life, such as:*
- war
- revolutions
- depressions
- death
- animosity
- jealousy
- lies
- public enemies

• tragedies of all kinds
• natural catastrophes

A father must discuss the causes and effects of these conditions in life, and prepare his children to deal intelligently with them. He must inform his children about what is happening in the world.

Most children have radios, but they listen only to music. They are not interested in hearing about world conditions. Fathers must find ways to interest children in the problems of the world, and encourage them to work hard to be one with those who try to solve these problems in life. Even an animal does not release its offspring into the wild until it knows that they can take care of themselves.

k. *A father must make his children aware that there are people in the world who are filled with animosity and hatred.* He must explain how these negative emotions originate and affect life. He can speak about historical events, showing the results of hatred and animosity. He must also explain how these feelings can be conquered and a cooperative spirit can be cultivated between nation and nation, and person and person.

The existence of jealousy and what it does, and how to handle jealous people and protect oneself from jealousy must be explained to children by their father. The father also must listen to the observations of his child about these things so that the child grows and matures.

Children must not be forced into negativity. Children must not be made to feel that all the world is full of hatred and jealousy. A balanced viewpoint gives children courage and faith and enables them to be victors in life.

Tragedies and natural catastrophes should be explained to children by their father. He can tell them what wise people do in such conditions of life. He must tell stories about heroes who survived great catastrophes and tragedies and achieved great heights because of these occurrences.

l. *Another matter that the father should discuss with his children is sex and marriage.* He must explain what sex is and how to handle it properly. He must speak about friendships with the opposite sex and how to handle them properly. He must teach them about how to prepare for marriage and the responsibilities of raising children. A father can teach his daughters specifically what a male is, how men must be handled, and what dangers exist in relation to them.

Some parents tell their children only the negative sides of sex and marriage. Others make everything rosy. Children must be raised on facts, not exaggerations, so that they develop a balanced attitude. For some parents sex is play; for others it is a serious responsibility; for others it is a forbidden ground. Children must be raised to see things as they really are.

m. *A father should also speak about his wrong choices in the past and how he handled and corrected*

them. Once a thirteen-year-old boy came to me and said, "My girlfriend is two months pregnant. I don't know what to do, and she is almost going insane." His parents had thrown him out of the house. His girlfriend escaped to another family, and both later tried to commit suicide. Children must learn about sex and relationships in advance from their parents, not from watching late-night movies.

What would you do if your thirteen-year-old became a parent? Do your children have enough information and moral strength to protect themselves from such conditions?

n. *The father must talk about the beauty of marriage, the beauty of an integrated family, and the blessings of having children.* Some fathers are very busy or do not care about educating their children. Some of them are the presidents of many companies and have no time for their children. Others are already sorry they married and are indifferent to the future of their children.

There are also those who try to be the best fathers, knowing that the future of the nation, even the world, rests on the quality of its children and the values with which they are raised.

o. *Another one of the facts of life which fathers must teach is how to make money and how to spend it wisely.* Children must be taught about money by their fathers.

p. *A father can teach his children that work and labor are sacred* and that they are necessary for their health, prosperity, sanity, and achievements. A father must not be an example of idleness, inertia, or apathy but of constant labor. An excellent proverb says, "The working iron shines."

q. *A father must introduce ideas about death* to his children as it happens around them. He can speak about it when their pets die or when they find dead birds or bugs. He should speak about it when friends or relatives die or are close to dying. He can introduce to them theories from various religions and philosophies without fanaticism or bigotry, and let the children choose the way they want to think. It is very important to explain to them about the Laws of Reincarnation and Karma, by which they can solve many obscure problems in their lives.

A father should help his children realize that one day he and their mother will die, and that it is good to learn to stand on their own feet. He must explain also to his children that they themselves will die someday, but that life does not end at the gate of death. A father must not try to prove immortality to his children. If the children have any memory from the Subtle Worlds, proof is not necessary. Almost eighty percent of children under age five have such memories and accept the reality of immortality.

A child must not be exposed to the world totally unaware of what is going on, but he should be given a logical approach to deal with the facts of life. He must always feel that problems exist, but that it is possible to solve them for the advantage of all humanity.

As a father introduces ideas into the minds of his children, he should not act as the authority but make his children realize that he is also a searcher, open to new ideas and approaches.

Fathers and mothers must present visions to the souls of their children. A father must inspire his children to continual service, creativity, and great spiritual achievements. He must bring to their attention the essentials of life and inspire them to dedicate themselves to bringing Beauty, Goodness, Righteousness, Joy, and Freedom to society.

ɪ. *A father must talk to his children about virtues, what they do to an individual, and how they create the future.* He must talk about those who lived a virtuous life, did great things in the world, and became good examples for thousands. He must discuss ways to cultivate virtues and how to use them in daily life. A father will not just speak about these things but will be a living example of virtue for his children. Children understand examples better than words. When children know about virtues and their effects, they will naturally strive to cultivate them and keep away from vices.

A father must also discuss with his children spiritual subjects. Spirituality is a progressive search for the cause of all that exists and for the laws governing all that exists; it is living in harmony with the cause and its laws.

To be spiritual does not mean to go to church or read sacred books or sing psalms. Whenever we limit the consciousness of children with special religions, traditions, dogmas, and doctrines, we stop their spiritual growth.

Children must approach the mystery of life without prejudice or superstitions. They must have respect toward all forms of worship, as long as they are within the boundaries of Beauty, Goodness, Righteousness, Joy, and Freedom.

Spirituality is a search for the Supreme Cause. It is living a life for the benefit of all and striving toward perfection.

A father is like the guardian angel of his children. He must cultivate the best flowers in them and protect them from every possible danger until they are mature enough to stand on their own feet.

About the Author

Torkom Saraydarian (1917 – 1997) was born in Asia Minor. Since childhood he was trained in the Teachings of the Ageless Wisdom.

He visited monasteries, ancient temples, and mystery schools in order to find the answers to his questions about the mystery of man and the Universe.

He lived with Sufis, dervishes, Christian mystics, and masters of temple music and dance. His musical training included the violin, piano, oud, cello, and guitar. It took long years of discipline and sacrifice to absorb the Ageless Wisdom from its true sources. Meditation became a part of his daily life, and service a natural expression of his soul.

Torkom Saraydarian dedicated his entire life to the service of his fellow man. His writings and lectures and music show his total devotion to the higher principles, values, and laws that are present in all world religions and philosophies. These works represent a synthesis of the best and most beautiful in the sacred culture of the world. His works enrich the foundational thinking on which man can construct his Future.

Torkom Saraydarian wrote a large number of books, many of which have been published. All of his books will continue to be published and distributed. A few have been translated into Armenian, German, Italian, Spanish, Portuguese, Greek, Dutch, and Danish.

He left a rich legacy of writings and musical compositions for all of humanity to enjoy and benefit from for many years to come.

Visit our web site at *www.tsg-publishing.com* for interviews and additional information on Torkom Saraydarian.

Other Books by Torkom Saraydarian

- The Ageless Wisdom
- The Aura
- Battling Dark Forces
- The Bhagavad Gita
- Breakthrough to Higher Psychism
- Buddha Sutra — A Dialogue with the Glorious One
- Challenge for Discipleship
- Christ, The Avatar of Sacrificial Love
- A Commentary on Psychic Energy
- Cosmic Shocks
- Cosmos in Man
- The Creative Fire
- Dynamics of Success
- Education as Transformation, Vol. I
- Education as Transformation, Vol. II
- The Eyes of Hierarchy—How the Masters Watch and Help Us
- Flame of Beauty, Culture, Love, Joy
- The Flame of the Heart
- From My Heart — Volume I (Poetry)
- Hiawatha and the Great Peace
- The Hidden Glory of the Inner Man
- I Was
- Joy and Healing
- Karma and Reincarnation
- Leadership Vol. I
- Leadership Vol. II
- Leadership Vol. III
- Leadership Vol. IV
- Leadership Vol. V
- Legend of Shamballa
- The Mystery of Self-Image
- The Mysteries of Willpower
- New Dimensions in Healing
- Olympus World Report… The Year 3000
- One Hundred Names of God
- Other Worlds
- The Psyche and Psychism
- The Psychology of Cooperation and Group Consciousness
- The Purpose of Life
- The Science of Becoming Oneself
- The Science of Meditation
- The Sense of Responsibility in Society
- Sex, Family, and the Woman in Society
- The Solar Angel
- Spiritual Regeneration
- Spring of Prosperity
- The Subconscious Mind and the Chalice
- Symphony of the Zodiac
- Talks on Agni
- Thought & the Glory of Thinking
- Triangles of Fire
- Unusual Court
- Woman, Torch of the Future
- The Year 2000 & After

Booklets

- The Art of Visualization — Simply Presented
- The Chalice in Agni Yoga Literature
- Cornerstones of Health
- A Daily Discipline of Worship
- Discipleship in Action
- Duties of Grandparents
- Earrings for Business People
- Earthquakes and Disasters — What the Ageless Wisdom Tells Us
- Fiery Carriage and Drugs
- Five Great Mantrams of the New Age
- Hierarchy and the Plan
- How to Find Your Level of Meditation
- Inner Blooming
- Irritation — The Destructive Fire
- Mental Exercises
- Nachiketas
- New Beginnings
- Practical Spirituality
- Questioning Traveler and Karma
- Saint Sergius
- Synthesis

Booklets
(Excerpts and Compilations)

- Angels and Devas
- Family Relations
- Courage
- Daily Spiritual Striving
- First Steps Toward Freedom

- Prayers, Mantrams, and Invocations
- Cooperation
- Responsibility
- Responsibilities of Fathers
- Responsibilities of Mothers
- Success
- Women as Torchbearers
- The Heart of Your Partner

Videos

- The Seven Rays Interpreted
- Why Drugs Are Dangerous
- Lecture Videos by Author (list available)

Music

- A Touch of Heart (CD only)
- Dance of the Zodiac
- Far Horizons
- Fire Blossom
- Go In Beauty (songs by Torkom Saraydarian sung by choir)
- Infinity
- Lao Tse
- Light Years Ahead
- Lily in Tibet
- Misty Mountain
- Piano Composition
- Rainbow
- Spirit of My Heart
- Sun Rhythms
- Tears of My Joy
- Toward Freedom
- 1994 Annual Convention Special Edition — Synthesizer Music

About the Publisher

T.S.G. Publishing Foundation, Inc. is a non-profit, tax exempt organization. Founded on November 30, 1987 in Los Angles, California, it relocated to Cave Creek, Arizona on January 1, 1994.

Our purpose is to be a pathway for self-transformation. We are fully devoted to publishing, teaching, and distributing the creative works of Torkom Saraydarian.

Our bookstore in Cave Creek and our online bookstore at our web site *www.tsg-publishing.com* offer the complete collection of the creative works of Torkom Saraydarian for sale and distribution. Our newsletter OUTREACH contains thought-provoking articles excerpted from these books. We also conduct weekly classes, special training seminars, and home study meditation courses.

Torkom Saraydarian
Book Publishing Fund

Torkom Saraydarian dedicated his entire life to serving others in their spiritual growth. At the time of his passing, more than 100 manuscripts had been written and prepared for publication. This work represents a seamless tapestry of Wisdom and we are dedicated to publishing the entire collection.

Torkom Saraydarian had the unique wisdom and dedication to write all of these magnificent books in one lifetime. Now it is our turn to do the work. Together we can make his dream a reality and bring his legacy to fruition.

We depend on contributions for the publishing of the books. A special fund, *The Torkom Saraydarian Book Publishing Fund* has been established for the completion of this legacy. Contact us for details about the *Book Fund* and an update regarding remaining manuscripts. You can contribute funds for an entire book, or give any amount you wish on a continuous basis or a one-time contribution.

Thank you for your loving and continuous support.

Participate in the Vision for the Future
Contribute to
The Torkom Saraydarian
Book Publishing Fund

My Pledge:

❑ One-time: $ ____ ❑ Annually: $ ____ ❑ Monthly: $ ____

Name: _____

Address: _____

City / State: _____ Country: _____

Tel #: (____) _____ – _____

E-mail Address: _____

Method of Payment: ❑ Check/U.S. Money-order ❑ Visa ❑MasterCard

Account # _____ – _____ – _____ Exp. date: ____ / ____

(If using credit card, please include account number & expiration date)

Please send to:
T.S.G. Publishing Foundation, Inc. • Attn: Book Fund
P.O. Box 7068 • Cave Creek, AZ 85327 • U.S.A.
Tel: (480) 502-1909 • Fax: (480) 502-1909
Web site: *www.tsg-publishing.com*
E-mail: *webmaster@tsg-publishing.com*
T.S.G. Publishing Foundation, Inc. is a tax-exempt, non-profit organization.

❑ I would like to pay for the publishing of a book in its entirely.
(Please tell us what you want on the dedication page.)

Ordering Information

Write to the publisher for additional information regarding:

— Free catalog of author's books and music tapes

— Complete list of lecture tapes and videos
($2 postage for each list)

— Placement on mailing list for continuous updates

— A free copy of our newsletter *Outreach*

— **Join our Book Club at no charge. (Receive a 20%
discount with each new release by Torkom Saraydarian. Each
new book is mailed to you automatically as soon as it is
released.) Send us a written approval to include you in the
Book Club.**

Additional copies of *Responsibilities of Fathers*
U.S.$4.50

Postage within U.S.A. – $2.50 plus applicable state sales tax
International postage: contact us for surface or air rates.

T.S.G. Publishing Foundation, Inc.
P.O. Box 7068
Cave Creek, AZ 85327–7068
United States of America
TEL: (480) 502–1909
FAX: (480) 502–0713
E-Mail: webmaster@tsg-publishing.com
Web-site: www.tsg-publishing.com